The Year's Most Worthy

W. Luke Suttles

Cover design: Luke Suttles
Edited by: Elizabeth Suttles

Unless otherwise indicated, Scripture quotations are taken from the KJV.

DEDICATION

To my family – those who still stand with me in this life
and, more especially, in the way to the New Jerusalem.
Their names are known to the Lord and to my heart.

.

CONTENTS

FOREWORD

A little more than five years ago, the Pastor of our church made what was, in our day at least, a novel proposition. A student of church history will quickly notice, however, that his proposition was in no way novel to the churches of a previous age. His proposition was this: that we come together as a church and, if possible, with other churches or individual believers, at the first of each year, to hold a New Year's service.

This service would be solely for the purpose of taking stock of the past year's failings and blessings and for preparing our hearts and minds for the coming year. There would be prayer; there would be some singing. But the centerpiece would be the preaching of the Word. And not just any preaching. And not just one preacher. In fact, there would be two or more speakers; and the messages were to take the form of admonitions; that is to say, they were to be calculated, as Mr. Webster has stated it, to counsel against a fault, to caution, and to instruct in some duty (see Webster's 1828 Dictionary).

The texts were to be chosen by the individual speakers. The particular topic to be treated from each text was to be settled on by each speaker. The only restriction set by the Pastor was that of time. Each speaker was to be given a set period of time in which to speak. That period would range from as little as eight to twenty minutes. Restricting the time allotted to each speaker in this way served two purposes. It prevented the service as a whole from being unusually long, as it might have been if multiple speakers each spoke as long as an ordinary sermon. But more than this, the time restrictions forced the speaker to make the maximum use of each minute to press home with clarity and power the message at hand – to distill the intended instruction to the fewest and most powerful expressions which might then, by grace, be more easily kept in the memory and written upon the heart. The goal was, after all, to furnish the hearer with some nugget or tool by which to be more faithful in the coming new year.

This little volume is the product of my involvement in the first five years of those New Year's services. The unusual and varied lengths of the messages are a result of the time constraints given to me each year. Moreover, it must be kept in mind that these admonitions were originally prepared to be delivered in person and not in book form, and so the style and arrangement is more akin to a speech than to a commentary or a formal study of these Bible passages.

As any preacher or teacher of the Word will know, the Master chiseled my rough edges by these very admonitions long before I was called upon to deliver them to the Church. And it is my prayer that the Lord will be pleased to use these "little speeches" to bolster and encourage, correct and instruct some other believers long after my days. And may the Potter get all the glory from the clay!

W. Luke Suttles, 2018

1

The Year's Most Worthy Effort

January, 2014

O love the Lord, all ye his saints: for the Lord preserveth the faithful, and plentifully rewardeth the proud doer.   **Psalms 31:23**

It is in our nature to love. God, Who is love, has designed our souls to love and to give love. This past year, some thing or other, some persons or other, have been the target of your affections. It is equally true that the object of your greatest love may not have been a person or a thing. It may have been an idea or a feeling. Yet, you have loved something. Love is a universal gesture among men. But while it is not a matter of *whether* we will love, it *is* a matter of *how* we will love.

And thus we find that when the Holy Spirit describes mankind in His Bible, He describes them as being those who either love the darkness[1] or that love His law.[2] They are those who love

---

[1] John 3:19: *And this is the condemnation, that light is come into the world, and men loved darkness rather than light, because their deeds were evil.*

[2] Psalms 119:165: *Great peace have they which love thy law: and nothing shall offend them.*

evil[3] or that love the good.[4] They are those who are lovers of themselves or lovers of God.[5] In a word, we are lovers!

So, as I stand before you today, I have no intention of trying to convince you to love, this coming year. I have no need of urging you to set your affections upon one thing or another. You will.

But, in keeping with the purpose of this gathering – a purpose to admonish one another in the service of the Lord – I stand today to urge you, in the words of our passage, to love your God![6]

This is the most fundamental need and requirement for all mankind. And so, when the scribe asked our Lord what was the most important commandment of all, He said, in those often repeated and seldom lived words, "Thou shalt love the Lord thy God with all thy heart, and with all thy soul, and with all thy mind, and with all thy strength: this is the first

----

[3] Micah 3:2: *Who hate the good, and love the evil; who pluck off their skin from off them, and their flesh from off their bones.*

[4] Amos 5:15: *Hate the evil, and love the good, and establish judgment in the gate: it may be that the Lord God of hosts will be gracious unto the remnant of Joseph.*

[5] 2 Timothy 3:2: *For men shall be lovers of their own selves, covetous, boasters, proud, blasphemers, disobedient to parents, unthankful, unholy.*

[6] Psalms 31:23a: *O love the Lord, all ye his saints…*

commandment."[7] This is every man's duty!

It is every man's duty, because He is every man's God. But it is more than simply His right as a Creator that demands men's love. His common grace is over every man. He causes His sun to shine upon the evil and the good. He provides even the breath needed for the wicked to curse His name. He is mighty and wise, merciful and good, full of pity and excellent in holiness. He is superb in all His ways! And every turn on the road of human experience brings us before another evidence of one or all of these His features.

So the Psalmist says: "Kings of the earth, and all people; princes, and all judges of the earth: Both young men, and maidens; old men, and children: Let them praise the name of the Lord: for His name is excellent; His glory is above the earth and heaven."[8] The simple fact is that He deserves your love, just because of who He is.

But our verse today, is more narrow than this. It addresses, not all men, but you who say you belong to Christ. *All ye His saints.* (vs.23) And just as the address is not general but particular, so the motivations that are given in this verse for loving Him are particular. Listen to the verse. (vs.23)

At the end of the day, no matter what the frustration is or the sadness or the anxiety, what

---

[7] Mark 12:30

[8] Psalms 148:11-13

message is fail proof medicine for the heart of faith? It is that God is a rewarding God! There is a fruit for labor and an answer to rebellion. It is that "He is a rewarder of them that diligently seek Him."[9]

But it is even more than that! The soul of a real saint could not be refreshed by only this, because this is only partial justice. Holiness is only fully satisfied by full justice; and so when the Lord wishes to comfort or admonish His people, He also reminds them that "the great God that formed all things both rewardeth the fool, and rewardeth transgressors."[10] He will repay tribulation to those who trouble His people, and to those who are troubled, rest![11]

Love the Lord, saint! But, why? Because, He *will* reward your faithfulness; and He *will* sufficiently deal with your every enemy! See how a worthy God makes Himself even more precious in the eyes of the saint? The faithful He does and will preserve, keeping them even as "the apple of His eye";[12] so that they can say about Him, like

---

[9] Hebrews 11:6: *But without faith it is impossible to please him: for he that cometh to God must believe that he is, and that he is a rewarder of them that diligently seek him.*
[10] Proverbs 26:10
[11] 2 Thessalonians 1:6-7: *Seeing it is a righteous thing with God to recompense tribulation to them that trouble you; And to you who are troubled rest with us, when the Lord Jesus shall be revealed from heaven with his mighty angels.*
[12] Psalms 17:8: *Keep me as the apple of the eye, hide me under the shadow of thy wings.*

the writer of the sacred Song of Solomon 2:3, "As the apple tree among the trees of the wood, so is my beloved among the sons. I sat down under his shadow with great delight, and his fruit was sweet to my taste."

Oh, why? Why this past year have we forgotten our Lord so very often? Why this past year did we love this world so much? Why did we long for the comforts and pleasure of the flesh so often? Why did we give so little of our heart to Him? How could we turn our shoulders to the only One who can promise such reward and really give it?

What do we think we are doing when we wrap our love around bits of dust and scorn a precious Lamb who whispers from the throne, "Come away with Me"? You have not "seen, nor ear heard, neither have entered into the heart of man, the things which *I* have prepared for them that love *Me*."[13]

Love the Lord, all people! Yes, and all people should. But, saint of God, if Christ, having set His love upon you before the world began, did then bleed and die to redeem your filthy soul, how much more ought you to adore Him with "all of your heart and mind"![14] How much more

---

[13] 1 Corinthians 2:9: But as it is written, Eye hath not seen, nor ear heard, neither have entered into the heart of man, the things which God hath prepared for them that love him.
[14] Matthew 22:37: Jesus said unto him, Thou shalt love the Lord thy God with all thy heart, and with all thy soul, and with

ought we to be in love with Him who loved our souls enough to overpower our justly earned penalty with His own suffering! Can you think of anything more worthy for you to do with every day this coming year than to give your strength to the full adoration and humble reverence of the Lord, the Savior of His people?

We ought to examine ourselves this day! Search your own heart. Weighed in the balances, which thing or person or thought that held so much of your affection this past year can compare to Him? What is too precious to you to sacrifice for Him?

For some of you, it may have been a person. For some it may have been a place. For some it may have been a moment. For some it may have been a memory. For some it may have been a goal. For some a lust. For some a reputation. For some approval. For some money. For some health. For some comfort. For some glory. For some vindication.

But for all of us today, I would admonish you, on the authority of the Scriptures to count it all this coming year but loss "for the excellency of the knowledge of Christ Jesus my Lord"![15] "O, love the Lord, all ye His saints"! He cannot get

---

all thy mind.

[15] Philippians 3:8: *Yea doubtless, and I count all things but loss for the excellency of the knowledge of Christ Jesus my Lord: for whom I have suffered the loss of all things, and do count them but dung, that I may win Christ.*

more worthy. So, let us get more faithful! "O, love the Lord." Brethren, *this* is the most worthy effort you will make this coming year.

2

The Year's Most Worthy Warning

January, 2015

The wicked shall be turned into hell, and all the nations that forget God.   **Psalms 9:17**

I cannot ensure that you will attend another service such as this, but I can assure you that it is appointed unto every man once to die.[16] And I can assure you that for many that appointment is set for this coming year.

With that in mind, I would call to your memory that one year ago this day, I stood behind Psalms 31 and begged every listener to love the Lord with all their heart. And I say again: O, love the Lord; for He is altogether worthy of your love! O, love the Lord, I say! But today, I would remind us that there is still a place for those that *do not* love the Lord – a place called hell.

Today, I know that many saints have lost their sense of urgency about this place. I know that hypocrites still rest their souls on vain religion to save them from this place. I know

_____

[16] Hebrews 9:27: *And as it is appointed unto men once to die, but after this the judgement.*

that sinners still grope in ignorance while headed for this place. And today, because I know the church is home to each of these kind of people, I am not ashamed to punctuate our peaceful celebration with a reminder that there is a place called hell!

Maybe you have never thought of hell. Maybe you have thought of hell, only briefly, and imagine that your religion will banish it from your experience. Maybe, like a big band in a tiny room, the sound of hell has consumed your guilty mind. Or, perhaps, because of your salvation by the grace of God, you have peace that you will never go to hell; but your Jonah's heart couldn't care less about a dying world.

It's possible today that hell is just a religious fable on the shelf of your mind. It's possible that hell is another dusty volume in your library of Bible terminology. But then, it's possible today that hell is the great tormentor of your days, harassing you before you have arrived because its language of guilt is all that's spoken in your unconverted soul.

Whatever the case may be in your life today, I would admonish you, with every bit of earnestness that I have, to take hold of hell! Confront it, I mean, as you find it in the Bible, while you still have breath to do so.

Take hold of hell, I said, as a reality spoken of by Jesus more than any other person in the Bible. Take hold of hell as the original cemetery of your soul and the grand enemy of life. Take hold of hell as the real conclusion of every unpardoned sin, and God be pleased to let that understanding transform your behavior in this coming year. May it sink into your soul today that hell was, in 2014! Hell is, today! And hell will be, in the coming year!

And I would remind you, hell doesn't care whether you believe that. Hell doesn't mind if you ignore it. Hell isn't bothered by our apathy. Hell isn't offended by atheism or upset by our religion. Hell doesn't care if you live in denial of it. Hell grows hotter as you grow colder.

And hell is patient. It doesn't care how long it takes a sinner to get there because hell knows everybody is teetering on legs of dust and in a few short days will take up their abode in a house of worms.

Need I remind you, God has promised every unrepentant, unbelieving soul to hell? Hell is made strong by that decree – a strong man that cannot be robbed! Just because some sinners die in peace, hell isn't fooled into thinking it will lose its reward. Men are fooled by this, taking their courage from grass, because it withers quietly.

But, oh, if they could be in hell when such a sinner arrives, having left like a lamb only to awaken roaring like a lion! "Now is the joy they lived in, all turned to brinish tears, and resolute attempts to sin, turned into hellish fears!"[17]

[17] John Bunyan, *Sighs From Hell: The Groans of a Damned*

And what a place to fear, since hell is uniquely suited to the damned! Matthew 25:41 calls it "prepared" for the Devil and his angels. My friend, God put thought into hell! He actually designed a place for the wicked to stay. While their rebellion knew no bounds on earth, neither did His imagination know any bounds in preparing them an answer – a place where the burning can only be described as a lake of fire, where the only light is in the memory of a writhing conscience, and on every heavy chain is stamped the word *Forever*!

Oh, that suffocating master of all torments in hell – this thing called *forever*! "That little word," says Mr. Watson, "quite breaks the heart!"[18] Truly this is the greatest tragedy of hell – what goes to hell, stays in hell! Maybe the worst affliction could be endured if the ages had an end; but what will it be to *stay* in hell!

There'll be no Bibles there! No preachers there! No times for peaceful examination of the gospel there! No space for repentance there! No Savior there! No redeeming blood! What goes to hell stays in hell! Poor condemned souls – sooner will they count the stars by staring at the sun or drink the sea without a mouth than bring an end to their woe.

This is the destination of every soul not

Soul, ed. Dr. Don Kistler (Orlando: Northampton, 2011), 155.
[18] I.D.E. Thomas, *The Golden Treasury Of Puritan Quotations* (Edinburgh: Banner of Truth, 1989), 137.

covered by the blood of the Lamb – every soul, no matter how many they may be, because hell is never too full – never too shallow or too narrow for the perishing. On the contrary, says the prophet, the grave hath enlarged its mouth, without measure.[19] "Hell and destruction are never full," says the Proverb.[20] In a word, there is always room to go to hell!

Well, some people wish to know where hell is before they will accept it as a fact. Some say it's in the center of the earth. Some say it's on some distant, burning star, or some such notion. But, on the authority of the Word, I can tell you where hell is today. Hell is at the end of unbelief!

And there is always an end to unbelief, for every knee shall bow, and every tongue shall confess, says the Judge![21] Dear unbeliever, ask me where hell is today. I will tell you; hell is at the end of your life. Dear Christian, it is to us I am speaking first today. Ask me where hell is; and I will tell you; it is at the end of the unbeliever's life. Have you reached to save them? For some, 2015 will be their last.

_____

[19] Isaiah 5:14: *Therefore hell hath enlarged herself, and opened her mouth without measure: and their glory, and their multitude, and their pomp, and he that rejoiceth, shall descend into it.*

[20] Proverbs 27:20a

[21] Romans 14:11: *For it is written, As I live, saith the Lord, every knee shall bow to me, and every tongue shall confess to God.*

I know some object to this sort of talk. If we are concerned to see people drawn to Christ, they say, we need to avoid this frightening language and focus on the gentle love of Christ. But, my friends, Jesus knew no such dilemma!

Come to me, He said, so tenderly and lovingly. *I will give you rest!*[22] But, said the same Jesus, *except you repent, you shall all likewise perish!*[23] The trouble is we are more concerned with our own sensitivities, and so we decide that if we can tempt the lost with the love of Christ, we will never need to mention the rest. After all, hell is hard for us to look upon. Surely, the world won't listen to our message if we use these hard words. But where is the love for souls in this?

No, tell them, I say! And tell yourselves again! There is a blessed Savior whom to know is life itself. He is all love, and in Him is a world of peace and joy for a sinner made clean by His precious blood. Yes! But there is no such happiness for the unbelieving and unrepentant soul! "I am meek and lowly in heart," said Christ.[24] And so He is – and so He was, this Jesus of Nazareth, who went about doing good, we are told,[25] and laid down His life that His

---

[22] Matthew 11:28: *Come unto me, all ye that labour and are heavy laden, and I will give you rest.*

[23] Luke 13:3

[24] Matthew 11:29: *Take my yoke upon you, and learn of me; for I am meek and lowly in heart: and ye shall find rest unto your souls.*

[25] Acts 10:38: *How God anointed Jesus of Nazareth with the*

enemies may live.

But *never* did Jesus sacrifice His holiness to gain a friend, nor will He ever endorse a self-loving, unbelieving rebel just to populate the New Jerusalem! If you doubt it, see then His burning eyes upon the Pharisees that day and hear the Savior say to them, *Ye serpents, ye generation of vipers, how can ye escape the damnation of hell?*[26] Those that have trouble reconciling His just violence with His tenderness have failed to realize just how much He hates sin!

I will be unto them as a lion, said the same Lord, *as a leopard by the way will I observe them: I will meet them as a bear that is bereaved of her whelps, and will rend the caul of their heart, and there will devour them like a lion: the wild beast shall tear them.*[27] Why? Vs.6, *because* they have forgotten Me! "Samaria shall become desolate … they shall fall by the sword: their infants shall be dashed to pieces, and their women with child shall be ripped up." Oh, why this sadness? Vs.16, *because* they have rebelled against their God!

"I don't know, Preacher. That Old Testament God was different," some would say. But in what New Testament book do we find a description of the supper of the great God? And

---

Holy Ghost and with power: who went about doing good, and healing all that were oppressed of the devil; for God was with him.
[26] Matthew 23:33
[27] Hosea 13:7-8

what's on the table then? The flesh of kings and captains and all men both small and great.[28] And how does Christ feel about their wickedness? Every last one, we read, shall be cast *alive* into a lake of fire burning with brimstone. (vs.20)

Oh, this is horrible! Who can bear to think of such things? Yes! It's true. And it is that which I would admonish us to bear in mind this year. I beg you; go to your own heart and set about the work again of rooting out every ambassador of hell. Go to those children, to that spouse, to those neighbors, to the lost in the world and tell them, Flee! Flee the wrath to come!

Tell them! Tell them sin is an arrow shot at the eye of God, but hell is a sword run through the heart of sin. Tell them, "The man that wandereth out of the way of understanding shall remain in the congregation of the dead"![29] Tell them, "God will have a time to meet with them who do not now seek Him."[30] Tell them if you love them. Tell them, "It is a fearful thing to fall into the hands of the living God"![31] So the apostle says, "Knowing therefore the *terror* of the

---

[28] Revelation 19:18: *That ye may eat the flesh of kings, and the flesh of captains, and the flesh of mighty men, and the flesh of horses, and of them that sit on them, and the flesh of all men, both free and bond, both small and great.*
[29] Proverbs 21:16
[30] Bunyan, *Sighs From Hell*, 33.
[31] Hebrews 10:31

Lord, we persuade men."[32] Go testify!

Just so said the man in hell when he lifted up his eyes, "Father Abraham, send somebody to my brethren *to testify*"! It's not the word that means to tell them gently but the word that means to call out earnestly.[33]

Oh, I wonder how many people we have known who have died already and are crying out to us, even as we are gathered here, "Go and testify this year so that others may not have to come to this dreadful place! Tell them sin isn't worth the hell it earns!" And do as Peter did, Acts 2:40, "With many other words did he testify and exhort, saying, save yourselves from this untoward generation"!

In the time I have stood before you now, more than 1,600 more souls have left this world. When your clock strikes midnight tonight, dear listener, over 153,600 more people will have left this world today alone – 56,064,000 in 2014! Oh, and if Jesus didn't lie, many were called but *few* were chosen.[34] For, "Broad is the way that leadeth to destruction, and *many there be which go in thereat*"![35] How many of those souls just today will have gone to hell?

_____

[32] 2 Corinthians 5:11: *Knowing therefore the terror of the Lord, we persuade men; but we are made manifest unto God; and I trust also are made manifest in your consciences.*
[33] Luke 16:28: *For I have five brethren; that he may testify unto them, lest they also come into this place of torment.*
[34] Matthew 22:14
[35] Matthew 7:13

Here then is the year's most worthy warning: Remember hell! Remember hell! And may that memory sanctify your year, however much of it you may have. Amen

3

The Year's Most Worthy Reminder

January, 2016

Though a sinner do evil an hundred times, and his days be prolonged, yet surely I know that it shall be well with them that fear God, which fear before him: But it shall not be well with the wicked, neither shall he prolong his days, which are as a shadow; because he feareth not before God. **Ecclesiastes 8:12-13**

The benefits of the Christian walk are very unlike the experiences along the way. Along the way are pain, sadness, loneliness, rejection, persecution, betrayal, and hatred. And by these experiences we are tempted to have a low view of following Christ. By these experiences we are liable to have *no* view of heaven's glory!

But we insist on making our reason the gauge of God's success! And so we shuffle dejectedly from one moment to the other, bewildered and discouraged, fearful and mostly useless. Bearing the seal of the Lord upon our heads, we scurry about from providence to providence stamping "hopeless" on everything we see. Unwilling to say out loud that the general cause of Christ is hopeless, we nevertheless declare it to be so by agreeing with the Devil that everything the Lord is doing in *our* lives is past useless, beyond pointless, or far short of hopeful.

It seems to us that there is no success in any cause but the world's. While the wicked prosper, the righteous flounder. "They are not in trouble as other men," said Asaph, "neither are they plagued like other men."[36] Oh, we know too much Bible to allow ourselves to say that the cause of the wicked is the winning cause. The very thought calls to mind several verses I'm sure.

And then our religious friends are always handy with Christian clichés about Beulah land and the by-and-by and everybody agrees with "amens," because it's the thing to do in public. But, the truth is, very often, we just don't believe it.

If the disciples could have taken a quiz on the sea that night,[37] they would have gotten the correct answer when asked who the Son of God was. They would have gotten the correct answer when asked if Jesus Christ could resolve men's problems. But until the carpenter from Nazareth finally hushed the storm, they just didn't believe it would be well *with them*! And yet I do sympathize with the doubting disciples.

---

[36]Psalms 73:5

[37] Matthew 8:24: *And, behold, there arose a great tempest in the sea, insomuch that the ship was covered with the waves: but he was asleep.*

Because the storm *is* raging! The battle does appear to be decidedly tilted in favor of the ungodly. Hell seems to make greater inroads into our courts, our congress, our congregations, and our communities by the day. And most confusing of all, some of our closest relations look like evidences that the cause of Christ is a losing cause. And all of this is not to mention the discouraging behavior of my own heart!

But today, let our troubled flesh be quieted by the Word of God – let our carnal reasonings be instructed by the voice of God. Listen again … "yet surely I know that it shall be well with them that fear God"! (vs.12) Oh, saint of God, why would He even have to send this word to us if it wasn't for that fact that we need the reminder that our God is not in the habit of losing ground? What a precious word to any struggling soul – everything's going to be okay!

That is, *if* you are a follower of Christ. Every day lost men and women take up this good Book in their hands and bathe themselves in the precious promises of God hoping to soothe their pain with a bit of divine cordial. But all the while they refuse to address the source of pain by an application of the law of God. These people are trespassers! And this promise is not for them, because there is no room in the house of comfort for those who do not fear the Lord their God.

Today we address ourselves to the encouragement *of the saints*. Today we address ourselves to the perseverance of the saints! I speak not to the sinner today who prolongs his evil ways. (vs.12) I speak not to the wicked today, who feareth not before God. (vs.13) I have no intention of speaking to your lot if you be outside of Christ, even though much and miserable is said about your sad plight simply by telling you how well it will be with the child of God!

No, indeed; two kinds of sinners do not belong here at this promise: that man who rages against the Lord, who presses on in his stubborn rebellion regardless of the warnings brought against him, who puts his mind to pursuing the lusts of his flesh and pushes his evil into every corner of every day God gives him *and* that raging fool that dares to contend with the King of heaven and imagines himself a law unto himself! These have received their souls from God in vain. Flesh is their god. "Their souls are only for salt to keep their bodies from stinking," as the philosopher has put it.[38] No, you that love vanity and seek after leasing,[39] this good word is not for you.

In life you'll have no solid peace; in death you'll be turned into hell; and in the judgement

---

[38] John Trapp, *Trapp's Commentary on the New Testament* (Grand Rapids: Zondervan, 1958), 326.

[39] Psalms 4:2: *O ye sons of men, how long will ye turn my glory into shame? How long will ye love vanity, and seek after leasing?*

you'll hear that awful sentence, *Go ye cursed into everlasting torment*![40] Your word is there, in Psalms 17:14: all his portion shall be *in this life*. Mark my words, my lost friend, your gains at best cannot be large, because your life cannot be long![41]

And tell the hypocrite he has no room here either – pretending that the Seeker of Souls can be fooled with a bevy of deeds and that deceiving the church on earth will ensure a place among the church in heaven! And, Oh, what a crowd of hypocrites we have today! Religion is all the vogue while the fear of God is treated like a plague.

But that's judgmental and arrogant, Preacher! Then the great Mr. Swinnock was equally deluded when he said, "There are … but few real Christians; many that flourish like fencers, beating only the air, but few that fight in earnest the good fight of faith. Godliness hath many complemental servants, that will give her the cap and the knee, a few good words and outward ceremonies; but godliness hath few faithful friends … [yea] many court her, but few marry her!"[42] No; this great horde of hypocrites – it shall *not* be well with you! It cannot be; for the promises follow only those

_____

[40] Matthew 25:41: *Then shall he say also unto them on the left hand, Depart from me, ye cursed, into everlasting fire, prepared for the devil and his angels.*
[41] George Swinnock, *The Works of George Swinnock*, vol. 1 (Edinburgh: Banner of Truth, 1992), 71.
[42] Ibid., 67.

who worship Him in sincerity and truth. All you who write your dreams in blocks of ice and carry them to hell, it shall *not* be well with you!

But on the other hand, this good word is for you, follower of Christ – for you that fear the Lord, the prisoners of hope,[43] the migrant bands of Christ-followers who have fled for refuge to lay hold upon the hope that was set before you.[44] These and only these can say with Paul, "I now live … by the faith of the Son of God, who loved *me*, and gave himself *for me*"![45] You see the relationship? Jesus and me!

These are the only ones who may say, "surely *I know* … that it shall be well *with me*!" This they can say because the words of the Master make them bold to claim it: "He that hath my commandments and keepeth them, he it is that loveth me: and he that loveth me shall be loved of my Father, and I will love him."[46]

But maybe your faith is weak and your

---

[43] Zechariah 9:12: *Turn you to the strong hold, ye prisoners of hope: even today do I declare that I will render double unto thee.*

[44] Hebrews 6:18: *That by two immutable things, in which it was impossible for God to lie, we might have a strong consolation, who have fled for refuge to lay hold upon the hope set before us.*

[45] Galatians 2:20: *I am crucified with Christ: nevertheless I live; yet not I, but Christ liveth in me: and the life which I now live in the flesh I live by the faith of the Son of God, who loved me, and gave himself for me.*

[46] John 14:21

assurance weaker, dear saint? "I hope it will be well with me, but I cannot be sure," you say. Mr. Simeon may help to clear up your sky. "It is this person alone," he says, "who fears God, that unites in his experience a dread of God's wrath, a [confidence] in Christ, and a love to the commandments."[47] Are these things true of you, dear listener? Do you stand in awe of the just wrath of God? Have you reached, at all, for the salvation that is in Christ, knowing truly there is salvation in no other? Have you any real desire to please the Lord by obedience to His commandments? Then, *surely*, I know it shall be well *with you*!

"Aye, I know it *may* be well with me. At least I know it will be well with some others," you say. Dear friend, have you set yourself to fear the Lord this year? Then, let me say, it shall be well with you! Countless lives of saints down through the ages can testify to the truth of this. But who could recount all the proofs from the history of the church? Will you consider rather the Word of God?

There, we will find a discerning God. I know the modern church sells a God that's made of men's imaginations. He is blind to any sort of distinctions – certainly distinctions of a natural

---

[47] Charles Simeon, *Expository Outlines on the Whole Bible,* vol. 7 (Grand Rapids: Zondervan, 1956), 378-382.

sort, but even of a moral sort. Why, He just sees all men regardless of position or behavior as one big mass of creatures that He loves with an unqualified love. But nothing could be further from the truth! Our God is a discerning God! He sees differences between people and He takes note of those differences according to how they vary from what pleases Him.

I would remind you, my friend, that as the Lord drew the Old Testament period to a close, he inaugurated the long, dark sobering silence that followed with these final words of resounding *distinction*! "Then shall ye return, and discern between the righteous and the wicked, between him that serveth God and him that serveth Him not"![48] Thus, leaving divine discrimination to echo through the centuries!

I say again; do you fear the Lord? Then He will put a difference between you and the world. It *shall* be well with you! "[He] hast made us unto our God kings and priests: and we shall reign on the earth"![49] This is His word to you. And know that He "loveth judgment, and forsaketh not His saints; they are preserved forever …[they] shall inherit the land (This land! All the land now polluted by God-haters and saturated with the blood of the sheep and lorded over by violent and rebellious men!), and [they shall] dwell

---

[48] Malachi 3:18
[49] Revelation 5:10

therein forever"![50] Are you walking in the fear of the Lord? Isaiah was sent to you, as well then; and the Prince has charged him thusly, "Say ye to the righteous, that *it shall be well* with him: for they shall eat the fruit of their doings."[51]

And then remind your hearts that the certainty of doing well doesn't begin with heaven. The Lord has bound Himself to righteousness in time as well as eternity; so we find in Deut.4:4 that of all the men that followed Baal, "the Lord thy God hath destroyed them from among you. *But ye that did cleave unto the Lord* your God are alive every one of you this day"!

And having begun such a good work, He will see it through so that if we run to the end of history we learn in the Revelation that when the "time of the dead is come … they should be judged … [and] that thou shouldest give reward unto thy servants the prophets, and to the saints, and *them that fear thy name, small and great*"![52]

Oh, saint of God! Can I encourage you to press on this year in the fear of the Lord? And can I build up your resolve at all with a reminder that your prosperity in the service of the King is a

---

[50] Psalms 37:28-29

[51] Isaiah 3:10

[52] Revelation 11:18: And the nations were angry, and thy wrath is come, and the time of the dead, that they should be judged, and that thou shouldest give reward unto thy servants the prophets, and to the saints, and them that fear thy name, small and great; and shouldest destroy them which destroy the earth.

deeply personal matter for Him? He says not that He shall relieve only your physical adversity. He says not that He shall only remove your persecution. He says not that He shall only vindicate your righteous doings among a godless people or that He wishes only to wash away your tears, and all of this as some distant friend or disinterested, benevolent King!

He says, instead, "Behold, I will make them of the synagogue of Satan, which say they are Jews …but do lie; behold I will make them to come and worship before thy feet, and to *know that I have loved thee*"![53] He would have the worlds to know, not that He intends merely to do you favors, but that He loves you!

Oh, these are wonderful and moving words, preacher; but how can I be sure it will be so well for me? From where I stand, my whole world is a mess. Every passing year is another iron nail, it seems, in the coffin of my hopes. The case just feels so desperate.

Dear saint, read not this: Surely I *feel* like it will be well. Read this instead: Surely I *know* it shall be well! Will you take Him at His word and refuse to believe the arguments of your carnal senses. Says Mr. Brooks, "It will never be well with thee, Christian, so long as thou art swayed by carnal reason, and reliest more upon thy five senses, than upon the four [Gospels]."[54]

---

[53] Revelation 3:9
[54] Thomas Brooks, *Smooth Stones: Taken From Ancient*

And here is how you may know it will be well with you, dear child of faith. This One Jesus spoken of in the Gospels! The One that you pursue – He is a King! Take a look at Him, and wonder not that it will be well with His children. Have you had a glimpse of what John saw? "Behold, the Lion of the tribe of Judah, the Root of David, *hath prevailed…*"[55]

Behold the regal Lord, crouched upon His covenant, who would identify Himself with you by springing from the loins of a murdering, adulterous Jew! Behold the God that died so that life might fall upon you who look upon His face in hope! What can He withhold from you, having not withheld His blood?

Oh, the grand things the Bible speaks of to describe the New Jerusalem or the beauty of the new earth! But when the Spirit would describe just how well it will be with the saint, He will only say, you just can't imagine! "It's [never] entered into the heart of man, the things which God has prepared for them that love Him"![56] So He simply calls it, "an eternal weight of glory"![57] I'm

---

Brooks, ed. C.H. Spurgeon (Edinburgh: Banner of Truth, 2011).
[55] Revelation 5:5: And one of the elders saith unto me, Weep not: behold, the Lion of the tribe of Juda, the Root of David, hath prevailed to open the book, and to loose the seven seals thereof.
[56] 1 Corinthians 2:9
[57] 2 Corinthians 4:17: *For our light affliction, which is but for a moment, worketh for us a far more exceeding and eternal weight of glory.*

trying to tell you, our doubts make us stupid. Get a view of Christ in His Word and you may say, "Surely, I know it shall be well with them that fear God."

Dear saint, I know the failures and scars of these past hundreds of days can hang on us like barnacles, pressing down our hearts like an overloaded cart, stooped and riding low. But today, as we stand upon the threshold of another year, I would call upon us to pluck up our resolve, shake off the dust of this past year as we hitch ourselves to the providences that lay before us. Let us leave behind today all that is past and lean forward into the gentle yoke of Christ. And let us be assured, it shall be well with them that fear God! Yea, "surely I know that it shall be well with them that fear God, that fear before him"!

Has thy night been long and mournful?
Have thy friends unfaithful proved?
Have thy foes been proud and scornful,
By thy sighs and tears unmoved?
Cease thy mourning;
Zion still is well beloved.

God, thy God, will now restore thee;
He himself appears thy Friend;
All thy foes shall flee before thee;
Here their boasts and triumphs end.

Great deliverance
Zion's King will surely send.[58]

Shout, ye little flock, and blest;
You on Jesus' throne shall rest;
There your seat is now prepared,
There your kingdom and reward.

Fear not, brethren; joyful stand
On the borders of your land;
Christ your Father's darling Son,
Bids you undismayed go on.[59]

Surely, I know it shall be well with them that fear Thee!

---

[58] *The Psalmist: A New Collection Of Hymns For The Use Of Baptist Churches* (Boston: Gould and Lincoln, 1854), 539, #902.
[59] Ibid., 728, #48.

4

The Year's Most Worthy Examination

January, 2017

…and God requireth that which is past.
Ecclesiastes 3:15b

If an enigma, as Mr. Webster says, is *a dark saying in which some known thing is concealed under obscure language*, we have come in our passage to an enigma. It is known that there is no change in God and that He is not subject to time. There can be, therefore, no actual movement from a past to a present to a future for Him. As to His essence, there is only now. And yet, for us, who have our being in Him, there is no present, in fact. All is motion.

We are as a man who stands upon a riverbank to watch a boat. It is above him and then below him but never only before him. So says the poet: The present moments just appear, then slide away in haste, That we can never say, "They're here," but only say, "They're past."[60]

---

[60] Taken from Isaac Watts' poem: *Time, What An Empty Vapor Tis.* For complete poem see page 41.

But what concerns us today, is that moments past are yet not entirely gone. Every moment carries with it consequence, whether good or bad; and it is this which demands a review of our past. It is this that is hinted at in our mysterious text. God requireth that which is past! Or, if another, better translation is allowed, God seeks out that which has gone by.

Brethren, we have ascended to the brow of another year. Look forward we should. But looking back we must, first. And if we know the Judge will take stock of our past, can we not be admonished to do so ourselves, while we may? What about a review of …

I. Our Means

Three hundred and sixty five days now, a gracious God has ransacked His creation to attend to your physical comfort and healing and continuance. And these things we ought to recognize and wonder at. But let us judge as the Lord judges. What is the body without the soul? And what is time to eternity? So then what are provisions for the flesh in comparison to provisions for the soul?

And just look at the advantages to which our souls have been exposed! Just think how you have been born *after* a great Reformation so that you can have the Word of God in your own language, and been born in a land where the gospel message is free to roam, and given husbands or fathers or friends to help you in the right way – the way good for your soul. Think how you have been given a minister of the gospel to beseech you to be reconciled to God, to warn you of your danger and call you to repentance, to instruct you in the way of favor with the King. It cannot be overstated the value of these advantages to your soul, and you have had them in abundance!

Fifty-two Sabbath days this year you have to account for, and how many openings of the Scripture to you within those days alone? Well over a hundred! Has it made any difference to us? Are we more crucified to the world? Are you better at denying yourself? Are you less ignorant? And do you love Christ more? Or, do you love your righteousness more? Would Jesus say to you like He did to them, "Are ye also *yet* without understanding?"[61] Or would Paul say, *when for the time ye ought to be teachers, ye have need that one teach you again which be the first principles of the oracles of God*?[62]

Oh, let me urge us all to review the use we have made of the means – the means! – to see whether the advantage gained by them is at all in keeping with the value and the number of them! And be assured, as one observes, that if they have proven useless to us, they will certainly prove injurious to us; for God requireth that which is

---

[61] Matthew 15:16
[62] Hebrews 5:12

past! He will not wink at wasted means.

"Then said He unto the dresser of His vineyard, Behold, these three years I come seeking fruit on this fig tree and find none ..."[63] These three years! We focus on the cutting of the fig tree there. Why cumberest it the ground? But will you notice how the Lord takes measure of precisely how many seasons of waste were past? These three years! Sinner, how long will you despise the means? How many years? Saint, will you make a review of this past year's means? Then make a review, as well, of ...

II. Our Sorrows

Have you had real sorrow this year? If you have, you will need no help to remember it. How could you forget your time as a grape in the press, crawling up the Hill Difficulty; when every night had teeth and every day a claw; more dead than alive because of hope, capsized; when every dainty of the world tasted like sulphur and even the precious meats of the Gospel like withered grass. Who was with you then?

When the demands of His covenant promise to drain you of this world exacted blood, how could you pay, but by bleeding? And whose blood could you let for your sanctification, but your own? It was a dark path to take – a narrow and anxious path, a path of tears and trembling

---

[63] Luke 13:7

when your bones waxed older within you. Oh, *my soul hath it still in remembrance*, the prophet could say, and is brought low within me![64]

Maybe some days, maybe months of days your sorrows and distress filled up this year. Look at it again! Some days, I know, are so bitter, it takes courage to look again; but look! It's good for you to make a review of these things, for *by the sadness of the countenance, the heart is made better*, said the ancient preacher.[65] The world would have you shake it off and despise ever looking back. But God will make an accounting. And so should you!

Look and learn from your sorrows. Unless we are wiser for them, we are a waster of them. "It is an awful thing to come out of trouble," one has said, "for it always leaves us better or worse than it finds us."[66]

Oh, look again at how the Father carried you along. Did we not come to this day, despite it all? Having entered a cloud we feared would burst in terror we were verily drenched with mercy! Yes, it was a rod that came, but it came dipped in honey. Think how much of the world He rid you of by this. See how He can weave a cloak for

---

[64] Lamentations 3:20: *My soul hath them still in remembrance, and is humbled in me.*

[65] Ecclesiastes 7:3: *Sorrow is better than laughter: for by the sadness of the countenance the heart is made better.*

[66] William Jay, *Short Discourses: To Be Read In Families* (Harrisonburg: Sprinkle, 2000), 31.

heaven on His loom of pain?

Oh, make a review of your sorrows and see whether you be better by them. Mr. Cowper could look back and say, "Worlds should not bribe me back to tread, Again life's dreary waste; To see my days again o'erspread, With all the gloomy past." Are you closer to this testimony, too? Then, let us make an examination of …

III. Our Mercies

Few things stir up our resentment and anger like loading someone with favors only for them to ignore us and remain ungrateful. It takes very little of this behavior to incite us to leave off being kind to them at all. What then does the Lord think of us? While we are obliged to do good to all men, He is in no way obliged to do good for us. Knowing that He requireth what is past, should we not ask, *what shall I render unto the Lord, for all His benefits toward me?*[67]

Oh, His continued mercies, His restored mercies, His preventing and delivering mercies! A small exam will reveal that *daily He loadeth us with benefits*![68] A mind made sensitive by grace will be quickly overwhelmed in looking back to count the mercies of the Lord. How many times has He laid you to rest in His arms and fed you at His table or clothed you from His store? How often

---

[67] Psalms 116:12

[68] Psalms 68:19: *Blessed be the Lord, who daily loadeth us with benefits, even the God of our salvation.*

He has made up your lack and wiped your tears!

When you were low, He set you upon a rock. When in danger, He guarded you. When in sickness, He nursed you. See how He has given you all you need and more, but never so much as to destroy you. See how He has not left you alone among men, though never so befriended as to distract you with their approval.

Look back! Look back again and make a reckoning of His mercies! He has not forgotten them. So, put your mind to recalling them and paying up that praise that they deserve. *Bless the Lord, O my soul, and forget not all His benefits*![69] Ah, but our memories are treacherous, are they not?

We will not give due attention to what we do not recall. A help is required, as the Lord well knows. Even so, He commanded Ephraim: *Set thee up way-marks, make thee high heaps: set thine heart toward the highway, even the way which thou wentest*![70] So, set up monuments, be it physical or not, to keep a record of all God's goodness to you; and may it never be said again, if it may be said of you this past year, that *of the rock that begat thee thou art unmindful, and hast forgotten God that formed thee*![71] What an awful thing to say of a saint of God. Banish it from our experience, Lord! And, then finally, let us examine ...

---

[69] Psalms 103:2
[70] Jeremiah 31:21
[71] Deuteronomy 32:18

IV. Our Sins

What a task is this! Quite possibly the greater work is *admitting what is* sin than in numbering what we find. This is a close and hard business – a bitter business – and one from which we shrink because it has the effect of deflating our pride. And yet it's one we avoid at peril to our own souls, for the Judge seeks out that which has gone by.

But how quickly upon a review of our own sins do we become distracted, then strangely comforted, then altogether vehement and exalted in the flesh by a remembrance of the sins *of others* until we find it near impossible to be grieved at our own rebellion (as though dwelling on their sins somehow lessens the guilt of our own)! And yet, however well we are inclined to think of ourselves, I can assure you that we are blacker than we imagine. However well you think you have done in comparison with another, you have no cause to degrade them or exalt yourself. It was no less than the great apostle James who was constrained to admit in the plainest of words, James 3:2, *In many things* **we** *offend all.* And if James, then surely me! Surely you. And if I hurt all men with my sin, then surely my Lord I grieve!

Oh, it's true, Lord. *We have not served thee as we ought; Alas! The duties left undone, The work with little fervor wrought, The battles lost, or scarcely won.*[72] Truly,

---

[72] *Psalms & Hymns of Reformed Worship* (London: Wakeman Trust, 2006), #445.

were we each to know the other's sins this past year, we would cry: It is of the Lord's mercies that we are not all of us consumed![73]   Only because His compassions fail not.   Do we know the truth of this?   Oh, *enter not into judgment with thy servant*, begged David: *for in thy sight shall no man living be justified!*[74]

Listen now; perhaps, to this very hour, some of you have been anxious about everything in the world, except the pardon of your sins!   Perhaps you have been greatly perturbed over anything but your sickly love for Christ.   Perhaps you have been greatly distracted by everything but your love for the souls you are standing next to.   Will you pray for a different mind this coming year?   Do let us look back – back at our means, back at our mercies, back at our sorrows.   But let us not fail to look back at our sins.

Because an honest review of these things will *humble us*.   Like a stained linen makes a show of cleanliness in the poorest light, so all our garments appear spotless in the darkness of our own pride.   But if ever we will examine our behavior in the light of God's law - our hearts in the light of His love - we will be assured we have no cause whatsoever to cherish the high views we have of ourselves.

And an honest review will feed charity

---

[73] Lamentations 3:22: *It is of the Lord's mercies that we are not consumed, because his compassions fail not.*
[74] Psalms 143:2

among us, for how hard is it to think poorly of those we see to be little or no worse than ourselves in the eyes of God? There is a proportioned relationship here, says one, so that *We shall be tender towards others, in proportion as we deal honestly, and severely with ourselves.*[75]

But an honest review, finally, will *promote diligence*, as well, in this coming year – diligence to repay the Savior with a more earnest guard against vice and a greater effort for virtue. And anyway, what distinguishes the life of a good man from any others, asks Mr. Jay, "but a faithful investigation of his faults … an endeavor to make each day, a practical criticism on the past."[76]

Dear listener, we stand upon the threshold of another year. Before we enter fully in, look back. God requireth that which is past. And so, says Paul, *Every one of us shall give an account of himself to God!*[77] What of our means? What of our sorrows? What of our mercies? What of our sins?

[75] Jay, *Short Discourses*, 34.
[76] Ibid., 35.
[77] Romans 14:12

TIME, WHAT AN EMPTY VAPOR TIS

Time, what an empty vapor tis!
And days, how swift they are!
Swift as an Indian arrow flies,
Or like a shooting star.

The present moments just appear,
Then slide away in haste,
That we can never say, "They're here,"
But only say, "They're past."

Our life is ever on the wing,
And death is ever nigh;
The moment when our lives begin
We all begin to die.

Yet, mighty God! our fleeting days
Thy lasting favors share,
Yet with the bounties of thy grace
Thou load'st the rolling year.

'Tis sovereign mercy finds us food,
And we are clothed with love;
While grace stands pointing out the road
That leads our souls above.

His goodness runs an endless round;
All glory to the Lord!
His mercy never knows a bound,
And be his name adored!

Thus we begin the lasting song;
And when we close our eyes,
Let the next age thy praise prolong,
Till time and nature dies.

Isaac Watts 1674-1748

5

The Year's Most Worthy Animal

January, 2018

For to him that is joined to all the living there is hope: for a living dog is better than a dead lion …
Ecclesiastes 9:4-10

Four times I have stood before you, on the brink of another year. We have followed the pattern of our Lord in drawing with words dipped in honey, alternating with hard and piercing exhortations.

We were begged, at first, to love the Lord. We were faced with a hell that waits for those who do not love the Lord. Whereupon, we were lifted with a reminder that it shall be well with the children of the King, only to be shaken after that with the chilling news that God seeketh out all that is past! And worthy were these words from our God! But now, brethren, in our fifth year considering things of worth, I would draw down your gaze a bit, as it were, to a more immediate but still worthy consideration. I speak of your life, here, now, on this earth.

This is a call to embrace what and where you are. This is not a call to be *of* the world. But it is a reminder that you are in it! This is not a call to self-centered, self-gratifying, hedonism or fatalism that the world embraces. But this is a call to care for the present. And not the present only as a thing one begrudgingly endures to get to the future or away from the past, but a thing to be valued all on its own. We simply must be heavenly minded. But, we are not in heaven yet! God has ordained that life come first and ordained that we live it.

If, as some have observed, sin results from our inability to balance things properly, I would admonish us to balance this scale again. There is, in my view, a thousand versions of false piety. And some would have us to be tidy little Fatalists, Baptist monks, or rigid Stoics who chastise ourselves for any joy in the present and squander the offered delights of our King by insisting that holiness is to shut out as much of this life as possible.

After all, here is doom and corruption; and no child of God will embrace this life as much as wander around in various states of Zen reflection (so goes the mindset)! And so we do - defeated but not defeating, defied but not defying, dominated and not dominating, until the Lord removes us altogether and leaves the world and the people in it to their sad and pathetic end. What a bitter and gloomy people we can be!

What a sour and defeated people we can be! What children of Adam and Eve! But God has put us in a garden – a garden of life, and of every lawful thing we may freely eat. Is it righteousness to drop His gift in the gutter and sulk upon the doorstep until the show is over? I cannot think it is. Brethren, this is a call to life!

This is a call to embrace all that is good in life and by it to more fully round out that joy we may lawfully have and, not ignoring the balance that will for eternity exist between our physical experience and our spiritual journey, be rejuvenated in our persons, and so more prodigiously labor in that good work that we ought to do.

There are some who err in making an idol of this life, but I suggest that others err in making a mockery of the gift of life. Some err who worship the now, others err in making an idol of a day gone by or an idol of indolence while waiting for the day to go by. Do you crave to be what God has called others to be and fail to be what He has called you to be?

Who with an ounce of grace cannot adore the lions of God's church in all of history, but the Spirit of God has said to us, *better* is a living dog than a dead lion. The lion is superior in many ways to the dog, to be sure. But Solomon is not drawing a comparison of quality but a contrast of possibility!

The lion was. But the dog is. It may be the lion is majestic, but the dog is the Shepherd's companion. And, in this sense, the most worthy animal this year just may be a living dog. May I tell you about this living dog?

I. He Knows (vs.5)

He knows something. He knows he will die! What a transforming piece of knowledge is this! Can you imagine how ignorance of death would affect your zest for life? Easily. But what may loom over us to depress us, if sanctified by the Spirit of God, may serve instead to enrich our lives without end.

Let me say: I firmly denounce all fatalism that recognizes the unavoidability of death and teaches us to live out our ungodly passions to the fullest. *Carpe Diem* is the mantra of a fool. But I firmly denounce, just as much, the defeatism that teaches men that since they will battle more with sin and trial and disappointment and loss the more zestfully and productively they live their lives they ought rather to sit quite still until this whole frightening experience has passed.

Perhaps the perspective of vv.5-6 is needed for us. I submit to you that we ought to labor to make a mark upon history, hoping the Master will expand His kingdom thereby when we are gone. But may I say that we ought to expect to be forgotten!

Oh, this is humbling. This is hard. But this is the ordinary way. You will likely soon be forgotten. Can you tell me: (vs.5) What is a forgotten memory? I answer: It's a footprint that's eroded. It's the morning tide in evening time. It's not even the imprint of who you were. It is you, *entirely gone*!

But you say, "What about our projects? Do we not believe in the value of writing to propel our work through history?" Yes we do! But a cursory review of that history will remind us that it is the exception and not the rule that one man's writings will mold a multitude of people. More likely, we may hope to reach someone or other just as other's writings have reached someone or other of our little flock. Still and yet, even for the Greats, we know their writings, but what do you really know of them? But the real power attending what they said was in their presence, brethren, *when* they said it.

I suggest to you, that the greatest impact one may ordinarily have upon history, is that which they have while still among the living! Excepting Christ Himself, too many proofs of this exist. Why will the glorious cry "give me liberty or give me death" not incite the same upheaval today? In part, because it lacks the power of the man!

Christianity, you see, is first about relationships. (The two greatest commandments being love the Lord and love others.) Paul had a doctorate; and, so far as we know, he never wrote a book. He wrote letters to living people, and that only when he couldn't be there face-to-face. If you would most greatly impact a generation that will never even know you, impact the relationships around you now!

The lions may be dead. But you are alive. It falls to you, then, to shape God's church tomorrow first by the people you shape now while you live. Can you hear the shocking finality of these words: (vs.6) Neither have they any more a portion forever in anything under the sun!

This is your portion now. This life. So use it. And use it hopefully, brethren. As long as you remain and God is on the throne, good may be done. Listen to the word: To all the living there is hope! Dismiss your pessimism in the face of God's Word.

II. He Works (vs.10)

But our living dog, he puts his back into his work, as well. There is a lot worth doing, all the way from ordering your house to writing books for the generations to come, building families to building nations – physical and spiritual work.

The terms of engagement are there in the Hebrew. The sense is that whatever you may have to do, strain your capacity to the uttermost! Christianity is not for the half-hearted, see? Solomon reminds us (vs.10) that the grave will rob you of any more opportunities to get done on earth anything else. So, "since every man is going to the grave," says Dr. Gill, "…and every step he has taken, and does take, is a step to the grave; therefore it is incumbent on him to do all the good he can in life."[78]

The living may do that – good, in this life. And it will be you that has to do it. It is well and good to encourage others in a good work. It's well and good to send them your support. But the terms are these: thy hand and thy might! There will be no "*good and faithful supporter*"[79] in that day. It is the good and faithful servant who enters into rest from his labors.[80] "This," says Mr. Henry quite pointedly, "is a world of service; we are here upon business."[81] And for the work among the living, a dead lion will never do. We need a living dog!

But blessed be our gracious Master, it need not be a beleaguered and haggard dog. Brethren, I am convinced we have done a disservice to God's weaker saints by expecting them all to be Scudders and Judsons. We may have infected our own hearts with a chronic bewilderment. God calls some lions. He calls more of Solomon's

---

[78] John Gill, *Exposition of The Old and New Testaments*, vol. 4 (Paris: Baptist Standard, 1989), 610.

[79] Matthew 25:21: *His lord said unto him, Well done, thou good and faithful servant: thou hast been faithful over a few things, I will make thee ruler over many things: enter thou into the joy of thy lord.*

[80] Revelation 14:13: *And I heard a voice from heaven saying unto me, Write, Blessed are the dead which die in the Lord from henceforth: Yea, saith the Spirit, that they may rest from their labours; and their works do follow them.*

[81] Matthew Henry, *Matthew Henry's Commentary*, vol. 3 (Peabody: Hendrickson, 1991), 851.

dogs. What a wonder of mercy is this that the King has called us to be servants, but not galley slaves! To work hard, but not destroy ourselves in the labor. Even so, this living dog …

III. He Partakes (vv.7-9)

The Father has made preparations for His perseverance. It's thy work, you must do. But it's thy bread and thy wine and thy merriment you may freely use! He has lodged the blessings of faithfulness in your portion and offers you courage to make use of the joy He would have for you. I fear we set up a standard that is not the Lord's if we frown upon the enjoyment of our labors and scorn pleasure in the goodness of creation.

It is not being a lion that saves a man. It is being an obedient child. And the Father has commanded both a moderation in all things and a joy in the goodness of His hands. Of course, we rightly shy away from all of the abuses of God's prescribed enjoyments. In their efforts to gratify their flesh, multitudes would cry 'Jesus' while holding tickets to Vanity Fair. "Liberty, liberty!" they say. But Brethren, it is that balance of which we spoke. Let us regulate our walk by the Word of God and not by the abuses of others.

Realizing that the danger is real of my appearing to argue for greater laxness in the Christian walk, please allow me to rest on the wisdom of some of the lions that are dead. Allow *them* to carry this point for me. So says the Hebrew scholar Mr. Delitzsch, "From aforetime God has impressed the seal of His approbation on this thy eating with joy, this thy drinking with a merry heart. The assigning of the reason gives courage to the enjoyment but at the same time gives to it a consecration; for it is the will of God that we should enjoy life, thus it is self-evident that we have to enjoy it as He wills it to be enjoyed."[82]

Explaining Solomon's words, Dr. Gill insists that, "the whole agrees better with religious persons, who under distressing views of providence, and from gloomy and melancholy apprehensions of things, and mistaken notions of mortification, deny themselves the free and lawful use of the good things of life; in seeing there is no enjoyment of them in the grave and after death, therefore let the following advice be taken … nothing is better for a man to do (eat thy bread and drink thy wine with a merry heart) … which includes all things necessary and convenient, and which should be used and enjoyed freely and cheerfully; not barely for the refreshment, but recreation; not for necessity only, but for the pleasure; yet with moderation … and with thankfulness to God." And again, he says, "This is all the outward happiness of a man in this life, and all the use, profit, and advantage of his

---

[82] C.F. Keil and F. Delitzsch, *Commentary on the Old Testament,* vol. 6 (Peabody: Hendrickson, 2011), 759.

labors, to eat and drink cheerfully, to clothe decently, to debar himself of nothing of lawful pleasure, particularly to live joyfully with his wife, and enjoy his friends; this is the utmost of outward felicity he can partake of, and this he should not deny himself."[83] So to his congregation, Mr. Simeon explained how Solomon, "contends, that neither a cheerful use of the bounties of Providence, nor a prudent participation of the elegancies of life, nor a free enjoyment of conjugal affection, will at all interfere with our acceptance with God, provided our ardor in the pursuit of heavenly things be not diminished by them. With this St. Paul also agrees: For he says, that 'God hath given us all things richly to enjoy'; and, that 'godliness is profitable unto all things, having the promise of the life that now is as well as of that which is to come.' "[84]

But Mr. Henry plainly adds, "We must enjoy ourselves, enjoy our friends, enjoy our God, and be careful to keep a good conscience that nothing may disturb us in these enjoyments."[85] Even the austere puritan Mr. John Downame advised believers to moderately partake of walking, talking, "poetry, music, shooting, and such other allowable sports as best fit with men's

---

[83] Gill, *Exposition of The Old and New Testaments*, 608, 609.
[84] Simeon, *Expository Outlines*, 384.
[85] Henry, *Matthew Henry's Commentary*, 850.

dispositions for their comfort and refreshing."[86]

Brethren, perhaps I belabor a point. I only intend to demonstrate that I argue not for carnal Christianity, so called, but argue away from popish asceticism and an austerity that would hide from the world the joyous bounty of the Kingdom. Life is a precious gift. And it is not against the law of God to enjoy it while we serve the King! If it is a delight to have God as your Father, show the church; show the world; it can also be a pleasure to serve so benevolent a Master!

IV. Conclusion

I am aiming at encouragement today. I am aiming at lifting your spirits in the work that lay ahead of us. I am challenging you to lay hold of life with zeal. We serve a gracious Master; truly His ways are pleasant to such as run in His commandments. We are the children of the King! And we are alive! So, there is hope! Embrace this life and take from it all the good there is to be lawfully had. Embrace your life and do all the good in it you may lawfully do. Be hopeful. Be joyful. Be busy. Be fruitful. Be bold. Be focused. Be jealous of what God has given us!

Live life like you own it, because your Father does! To be sure, we are the only ones not

---

[86] Leland Ryken, *Worldly Saints: The Puritans As They Really Were* (Grand Rapids: Zondervan, 1986), 189.

trespassing on the King's good ground. Go to the Master like a lamb, but go to the world like a lion! It's ours by right. Did you not hear the preacher? Our Joshua has already gone in and taken it! It's ours by right of our Creator, but thanks be to Christ, its ours by right of redemption. So that every bit of joy, every bit of hope, every precious promise in it is mine.

Only I can really sing. Only I can really rejoice. Only I can have real and lasting courage. Only I can use reason aright. Only I can rightly enjoy nature. Only I can eat and drink and not eat and drink condemnation to myself. Only I can plow my fields without the Judge's fury. Only I can work with that fulfilling sense of real and lasting purpose. Only I can live down the dread of dying. Only I can boast a boast that doesn't go before destruction. Only I can live so as to die in peace!

Brethren, *there is a suicide that lasts a lifetime* – it's in wasting the life God gave you and pining for a life you will never have. You may not be a lion, my friend; but this year, be at least a living dog!

ADDITIONAL PUBLICATIONS OF COWETA PARTICULAR BAPTIST CHURCH

John Bunyan's The Holy War – An Updated Edition with Study Questions by Dr. Teresa Suttles

The Life of John Bunyan by Dr. Teresa Suttles

A Basket of Summer Fruit by Susannah Spurgeon (edited by Teresa Suttles)

A Carillion of Bells by Susannah Spurgeon (edited by Teresa Suttles)

A Cluster of Camphire by Susannah Spurgeon (edited by Teresa Suttles)

The Baptism of Believers Only by Dr. Thomas Baldwin (edited by John Gormley)

Meditations Among the Tombs by Rev. James Hervey (edited by Elizabeth Suttles)

Please visit our website for other books and resources:
www.cowetaparticularbaptist.org

96173840R00040